Warhammer 40,000 Space Marine Companion Guide & Walkthrough

kakrjup

ISBN-13: 979-8-8663-4419-2

CONTENTS

into the armor of a relentless Space Marine! This guide to Space Marine contains full game walkthrough with advices to every more difficult encounter and information about stronger enemies. Besides, quite big part of text is dedicated to items you can find.

Last update: 11 May 2016

This guide to Space Marine contains full game walkthrough with advices to every more difficult encounter and information about stronger enemies. Besides, quite big part of text is dedicated to items you can find. Localization of every 48 SKULL PROBES had been described with details and illustrated - thanks to that, you'll easily find and listen all hidden recordings.

In order to make using this guide easier, we introduce colorful fonts and special marks.

Legend:

Red color - guns, ammo.

Orange color - skull probes/recordings.

Green color - skills, important elements of game.

Bold font - used buttons.

[1], [2] - marks connected with screens. [1] is for the left one, [2] for the other.

Michal "Kwise" Chwistek

Walkthrough - 1 - Landing on the planet
WH40K: Space Marine Guide

Last update: 11 May 2016

After landing, you'll be quickly acquainted with controls. To move use W, A, S, D keys and mouse. Melee attack at RMB, shooting and LMB. Destroy first wave of enemies

When minor orcs died, there'll appear bigger ones [1]. Daze them by pressing F and then execute (E) - it'll regenerate your health [2]. You can reload gun at R key.

Moving straight, you'll be shot from the right by orc[1]. Aim him, pressing MMB, and kill. To do that, you can also shoot in explosive barrel at right[2].

Until further ne of fight - awaiting you[1]. During battle avoid center of location, because there hit a rocket missile, which cause lot of damage[2]

At the right corner you'll find next orc, standing near to barrel[1]. Blow him up, and go straight. You'll meet commander of opposite army[2].

Now your task is damaging orc's ship. At the beginning use fast and dazing attacks to exterminate running orcs[1]. To avoid being surrounded, make somersaults, pressing

SPAC L key[2]

After cleaning area up, you should move to anti-aircraft gun and use L button [1]. It turns in such way, that you'll shot down enemy ship [2].

2 - Against all - p. 1
W1140K - Space Marine Guide

Last update: 11 May 2016

Your next mission is finding Leandros and Sidonusa. Firstly go straight until you got to place marked pulsating fist[1]. Further road takes you to low fault. Jump down, and shoot out foes standing at the left[2].

When you arrived to crossroads, turn right. Blow up barricade[1] and go to the skull packet[2]. You can take by pressing -E and listen it, putting this key again. There is lot of similar stuff hidden in the game – its localization you'll find in other part of this guide. All gathered recordings you can listen in "Audio Logs" in main menu (Esc).

After collecting item, go back to crossroads and choose the last untested path[1]. Enemies which you meet shouldn't be problematic [2].

They'll defend container appellatives by racks[1], inside which you can find Bolter. Take it, putting E [2]. Guns can be changed by mouse scroll or at numeric keys.

Use your rifle to kill charging ones[1], and go to the place, from which you were attacked. Going straight look carefully at balconies. From behind one of those railing, you'll be attacked by two enemies[2].

Little further you'll meet a soldier, bravely fighting with horde of furious ones [1]. Help him kill enemies, hiding from occasionally in a corridor, from which you come in[2]. Foes will attack from above and under, so be careful.

At some moment the short cut-scene starts, little while after next enemies appeared [1]. Shoot them down, before they reach you. After battle search the room. You'll find boxes with ammo [2], which can be used by pressing E.

Going still straight you'll find system of trenches, and fighting soldiers far away [1]. Run to them by holding Left SHIFT and kill several ores [2]

Next enemies are right ahead [1]. When you finish then, collect ammo and go the place ticked by fist [2].

After short cut-scene run straight, until you find your lost companion [1]. Talk to him. You'll get a task: finding command bunker. But before you start that mission, walk to blue locker at the centre of plaza and pick up Chainsword [2]. Full list of combos to this powerful weapon you'll find in main menu, at Moves in fight.

Still going straight. You'll be attacked by many enemies [1]. Those standing downstairs kill by sword, the rest just shoot down [?]. A moment after you reach crossroads.

At the beginning go left. Just after the barricade [1] there is a box with ammunition.

which you can take. Turning right is a way to find new opposite team [2].

Smash all enemies and go on the top of trenches. When you walk up to the edge from right, bomb squad appears [1]. Blow him up and jump down [2].

Onward you'll be attacked by one similar creature and group of orcs. Just kill the suicider

- remainders died from shock wave

Few steps further stands chest with grenades [1]. Pick it up and throw into enemies, pressing Q key [2].

When you destroy the first ore wave, hide behind mantle at the left [1]. Find there ammo and grenades, which will be used to hold off enemy charges [2]. At the battlefield you should also look at red barrels. Blowing them up, you'll easily kill most of enemies.

At some point leader of ores will join to the fight [1]. It's elite enemy, but not very problematic. Firstly shoot to him from rifle, constantly hiding behind coverings, and finish him with combos. Chainsword [2]. You can also use grenades, if you still have ones.

When he'll be done, wait until the bunker's door opened and go inside [1]. At the end of corridor you'l find first cross lieutenant [2]

2 - Against all - p. 2
WH40K: Space Marine Guide

Last update: 11 May 2016

After talking with the soldiers leader, move to yellow locker in the corner [1]. Inside it is Purify Seal which unlocked Fury [2]. Fury rate increase, when your character damages enemies. When it is full, press T, it starts Fury state. Your attacks get stronger and every one will regenerate your Health. Fury is over, when Fury rate decrease to 0.

When you get friendly with new ability, follow the lieutenant [1]. Woman will take you to the vent and give new task. You'll have to go to the fortress, in which orcs hide a cannon. Going still straight, you'll be attacked by big orcs formation [2]. Kill them all you can do it too. Butter of Chaos road.

When everybody lied down, turn left [1]. Pick up ammo and grenades [2] and run straight, eliminating next enemies.

You'll get to soldiers post, where the Heavy Bolter is[1]. Use it pressing E and kill hordes of orcs [2].

If you want, you can take off cover at from stand, clicking RMB [1]. After fight listen what Leandros has to say and go further [2].

Your target is marked by pulsating red [1]. When you get there, go straight into ruins, you'll find another blue container, inside it the Bolter Hunter is hidden[2].

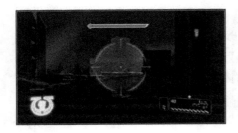

It is very powerful sniper rifle, which can be used to kill enemies from big distance. You can zoom clicking Left CTRL/MMB [1], and shoot on LMB. Armed in such way, make few steps and prepare to watch cut-scene [2].

After short film, turn left. Pick up ammunition [1], and go out at deserted plaza. Far ahead of you, first orc appear - shoot him down, using Hunter [2].

Second enemie is at the right upper corner [1]. When you kill him, three more orcs arrived. One downstairs, and two on the top of the ruins [2]. Few shots from Hunter should clear the place.

On right, from the place where one of enemies was standing, you'll find corridor appellative by fist [1]. Take ammo from the inside, and go straight, looking carefully at the ceiling. In one of holes you'll see a grenades throwing orc [2]. Run away from grenades, and kill him as fast as possible.

A bit further you'll arrive to big fault [1]. Jump down and eliminate charging goblins and ores [2].

Going straight, you'll see a hostage goblin, who'll blow up a barricade [1]. Behind it, is box of ammo [2].

A dozen metres onward, an army of orcs attacked you[1]. Kill all enemies and move up to fist marked door [2].

Pressing F you'll open these – go inside [1]. Corridor leads to next, similar passage. Open the gate and pick up Jump Pack from supply capsule [2].

To use it, hold SPACE [1]. Thanks to it, you'll be able to fly. When you press RMB during the flight, your hero makes powerful attack on the ground, which kill or stun enemies[2]. Unfortunately, pack decrease your distance fighting ability - wearing it, you can use only Bolt Pistol and Bolter.

With your new toy, get to the other side of the door, and kill all orcs standing on platforms[1]. Your comrades will take car about those standing downstairs [2].

When the last one are died, open the next door and repeat action [1]. This time, you can help two marines - there'll be lot of enemies downstairs [2]. After fight go into the cave, to which cables lead, and start next chapter.

3 - Rim of the Beast
WH FAK - Space Marine Guide

Last update: 11 May 2010

When mission starts, go straight, along cables [1]. Without problems, you'll get to the fortress with the cannon [2].

Pick up ammo [1], turn left and move to blue container [2]. Inside it you'll find Vengeance launcher.

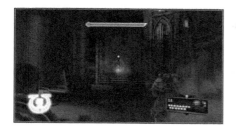

This powerful weapon shots charges tagging along to walls and armors, which can be detonated R-key[1]. Equipped in its school, go to the right corridor, and open the gate at end of it [2].

In next room are two gates - one with green diode, one with red [1]. Open the green one and go straight[2].

After defeating small orcs team, you'll get to the armory[1]. On the center of the room Thermical Bomb stands [2].

When you pick it up, gate will open, and you'll be attacked [1]. Kill him with launcher, and go back to the gate with red dolls [2].

It'll open automatically, and orcs appear [1]. When you kill the last one, activate the machine in front of you and use elevator to get on the lower level [2].

You'll get to the big hangar with ammo box [1]. At right will be next encounter with hordes of enemies. Try to fight on distance, because there are bomb squigs between them

[2]. If you move to close, they'll detonate – and you're dead.

Defeating first ore squad, open the gate at the end of corridor [1]. On the second side, there is another twice fighting enemy team. Get rid of them using your sword, and use mechanism on your right [2].

Nearby a bomb appears, on which you can locate earlier collected charge [1]. Press E key one more time and your hero'll push the bomb in proper direction [2].

Now, go back to the elevator[1]. Inside it, group of orcs and their leader are waiting for you [2].

At the beginning, get rid of these weaker enemies, and then focus on elite one. When he it get too hostile, choose the powerful one and attack with sword [1]. After a while, there should be an icon, showing possibility to execute him. To finish your foe, keep pressing E key as fast as possible [2].

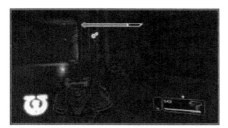

Elevator takes you on upper level - on the corridor you'll find big supplies of ammunition [1]. Pick up all of it, because behind the gate waiting for you more serious fight. Firstly kill charging enemies, and then, one by one, eliminate shooters hiding on upper platforms. Near to them you can see explosive barrels, which helps you exterminate green idiots [2].

Behind next gate, go straight. You'll get to another elevator [1]. But before you use it, search nearest room - there is a box of ammo hide inside [2].

On the next floor, kill gretchins and check yellow container [3]. You'll find Purity Seal, which unlocked Sniper Mode [3]. In Sniper Mode time slows down, which allow you to aim more precisely. To use it, activate Fury and press MMB.

New ability will be useful in the next room. When your companion starts to pushing a bomb, orcs appear on upper platforms. Activate Sniper Mode and eliminate them [1]. A moment later, on lower level horde of orcs, goblins and bomb squig turns up [2].

Kill all of them on distance, healing yourself by execution [1]. Among enemies one captain can be found - kill him like the previous one [2].

At the moment the second ores team come up, hide by nearest wall and kill rest of the melee fighting enemies [1]. Only when they all are dead, use again Sniper Mode and shoot down ores on platforms. After this long and quite difficult fight, short cut-scene starts. And then new stage [2].

4 - Graia's Titans
W1140K: Space Marine Guide

Last update: 11 May 2016

When the stage begins, go straight [1]. At the end of the platform, turn left and go one level down [2]. You'll meet few orcs there, but they won't attack you.

Moving left, you'll reach the big gate [1]. Open it pressing F and go inside the hangar [2].

The only one available path will lead you to the place with ammo [1]. At right from boxes is a barricade, you can destroy [2]. Behind it extra bullets are hidden.

When you pick up all useful items, go deeper into hangar. Far away you'll see a ram which you have to reach [1]. On the way to it, few orcs groups will attack you [2]. Fight them on distance, because there are Bomb squigs among them.

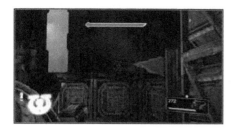

After defeating first group go downstairs and kill next ores. Bit later you'll find wide stairs [1]. When you get on the top, two enemies start shooting to you [2].

Get out of there as fast as possible, because a while later several sneakers start charging on you. As you reach high point [1], you'll get on train with him [2].

When you go through 3 big gates [1], you'll reach open part of vehicle, where you'd be attacked by the group of orcs [2]. Kill everything on your way and run straight.

At the end of the wagon you'll see one using Plasma Gun [1]. Shoot him down by Hunter. Go up stairs and start shooting from this powerful weapon [2].

Using it, you have to shoot down orc's craft flying over the train [1]. Shot only when vehicle is above you. If it fired on the flank, hide and regenerate armor [2]. Remember also about cooling down the cannon (R).

From time to time, from the craft will jump down team of enemies [1]. In that case run to your comrades and, behind the corner, kill all green scums [2]. Among them is elite unit, so I advise using Fury and execution as often as possible (healing). Amount of assaults depend on how fast you shoot down orc's craft. The worse your aiming is, the more encounters you will have. When fight is over, the next stage of campaign starts.

5 - Inquisitor
WH40K: Space Marine Guide

Last update: 11 May 2016

When you get off destroyed traтом, the cut-scene begins - you'll get word about mysterious inquisitor [1]. Listen to recording and move on to the second side of nearby storehouse [2].

Behind the gate you'll see a group of orcs, which you have to kill [1]. Once awhile new squad comes up, so be prepared for longer fight [2].

When the last one enemy died, go into the next hangar [1]. From its opposite side next foes start turning up[2].

Still shooting, look carefully for enemy's leader. This powerful enemy will charge at the moment he sees you [1]. Move back and use Vengeance Launcher. After few shots finish him with sword, and take care of rest of romp [2]. During the fight you can also use Fury, if you charge it before.

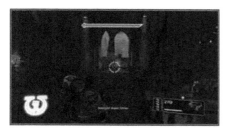

Killing next enemies, you'll move to controlling room [1]. It is full of orcs. Throw few grenades and finish the rest with rifle or sword. Look out for them leader, who can damaged you badly. Stun him, let him tastes a sword and execute [2].

When the room is clean, take ammo from the left [1], and use marked mechanism [2]. In that way, you'd destroy stolen cannon.

In further road move through the gate next to the mentioned ammo [1]. Downstairs are Ork are waiting for you. I advise to kill them from distance - there are few bomb squigs with [2].

After a while, you'll reach the place, from where you have to jump down to small trough [1]. Just when you do it, horde of goblins appears. Eliminate them blowing out nearest barrels.

Your next goal should be shooters standing upstairs [1]. When they died, take care of the rest [2]. Going straight, you'll get to the place guarded by green gunners. The best way to kill them is use Vengeance Launcher. Shot them behind a corner, and blow out all charges. A moment later you should reach the hangar.

Inside it run over the pavement [1]. You should see a hole, through which you'll get to the lower level [2].

After landing, you'll get an information about incoming orcs. Move up fast to the blue container and pick up Power Axe [1]. Thanks to that weapon, fighting becomes much more easier. Orcs will attack from everywhere, so use mainly close combat stuff [2]. Also, use rapidly the Fury. You'll regenerate it fast, by killing enemies. Use Fury second time, when two elite foes arrived. Due to that, eliminating them should be a piece of cake. Remember to hide behind mantles, it saves you from additional shots.

When the last creature died, go over to the platform - there'll be your comrades and other soldiers waiting [1]. Elevator goes down. When it ends, run straight and the next stage will begin [2].

6 - Lair of Giants
WH40k - Space Marine Guide

Last update: 31 May 2016

On the opposite end of the corridor, you'll find elevator [1]. Activate it - it'll take you on upper floor [2].

There will be a gate which you have to unlock, at the right [1]. Behind it, your companions check mechanism and confirm inquisitor's presence [2]. Listen to them and go downstairs.

Moving straight, you'll reach a platform, which you be able to leave using the proper mechanism [1]. You'll get into the room in which you'll contact with Midas squad [2].

After short conversation, go through the gate on right [1]. Corridor will lead you do the big factory room [2]. Few orcs inside shouldn't be a problem.

Going straight, you'll see next gate ahead [1]. Use the mechanism behind them, and go into the chamber in front of you. You'll meet there mysterious inquisitor [2].

Go to the next room with him - short encounter with orcs awaits there [1]. Defeat all greenskins and go out through the first marked gate [2].

In the next chamber go downstairs and pick up Plasma Gun from blue container [1].This powerful weapon relieves Bolter Gun. Using it you can shot weak missiles (LMB) or exploding balls (hold LMB). Move back upstairs and go further along the iron pavement. At some moment your path bars shaman [2], who will summon orcs with shields.

Daze them using key grip and finish with axe [1]. Remember about stronger missiles. At the end of the pavement is an elevator, which takes you underground [2].

Finely corridor leads to room with experimental energy source [1]. Wait until inquisitor opened inner chamber and go inside it [2]. A moment later ones come up.

Elite units will be among them, so use Fury very fast [1]. After defeating first squad activate the mechanism marked with rack [2].

Don't waste time on enemies - take standing in the centre core [1], and the mission is over [2].

7 – Heart of Darkness

WH40K : Space Marine Guide

Last update : 11 May 2016

After beginning a stage, go into the pits and run straight [1]. During the march you'll pass a small barricade [2]. Destroy it and pick up hidden ammunition.

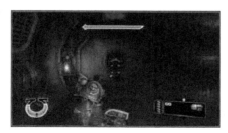

Tunnel leads you to the door, which can be easily opened [1]. Orcs are waiting for you behind them [2].

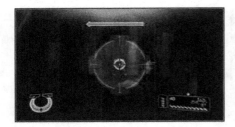

Firstly use Hunter and get rid of gunners on the platform [1], and then kill goblins via axe or sword. Make similar in the further part of corridor [2]. In case of any problems, use Fury.

After few meters path should get to the next system of tunnels [1]. Path will be very easy - don't forget about looking around - you can find a lot of ammo [2]. But be careful - there are suicide monsters falling off from ceiling.

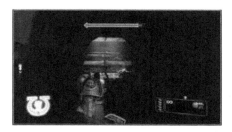

When you reach the gate, open it, and kill orc from the left rapidly [1]. On the right is box with ammo [2]. Moving forward, take care of single enemies.

Encounter with hordes of enemies awaits you in the bigger corridor [1]. Remember first to shoot your foes, and then go into close combat. Weakened opponents will be much easier to defeat. Save Fury for the second wave - there is close warrior in it [2].

When the last enemy dies, go into the tunnel on the right [1]. Moving forward, hold finger on the trigger. Once inside detonating creatures will charge on you. Next three will hide behind one with a shield [2]. Blow them ASAP, and finish meleed enemy.

Behind the gate you'll find blue container with new weapon - Thermal Rifle [1]. It's powerful gun, but its reloading time is long, and amount of ammo is low. Best to use against more difficult enemies. Little further, you'll be attacked by orc's army [2]. Weaker foes eliminate with Bolter and cold steel. New rifle use to eliminate enemies equipped in two weapons and armor.

Going straight, you'll reach high ruin. Jump off it and destroy barricade at left [1]. You'll find there ammunition and skull probe [2].

Stairs on the right leads you to the next gate [1]. Open it and go forward. There is an elevator inside big room with ores - it'll take you on the upper floors [2].

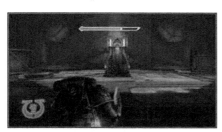

After getting into the place, open yellow container [1]. There is Purify Seal inside it - it lets you use now Powerful Fury [2]. Thanks to that, amount of Fury decrease much slower.

A moment later you'll fight against cultists [1]. There are many of them, so try to daze weaker enemies and heal yourself making executions [2]. To avoid gunners, fight behind wide pillars.

When opponents are gone, downstairs and run to the marked corridor [1]. You'll meet comrades there [2].

After short conversation open the gate on the left. There is a room with hordes of orc behind them [1]. Amongst them are new type of enemies - with rocket launchers. Try to kill them at the beginning [2]. Don't worry about Fury. This time you won't meet elite unites, so use it often.

After that, go upstairs through the demolished ceiling [1]. The path will lead you on the surface of the planet [2].

8 - Whispers of The Dead - p. 1
WH 40k - Space Marine Guide

Last update: 11 May 2016

When you get outside, move forward and go into the building on the left [1]. Corridor will lead you to the hole on the floor [2]. Jump down and run straight.

A moment later short cut-scene begins [1]. When it ends, come up to the blue container and pick up Laser Cannon [2].

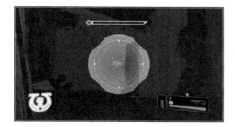

Use it to shoot down orcs with rocket launchers, who appears few steps further [1]. During the fight, hide behind mantles and try aiming enemies heads only [2]. It saves you lot of ammo - one such shot kills an orc.

When the fight is over move to the corridor in right upper corner of location [1]. Inside it, go straight, until you see soldiers fighting with orcs. First kill weak goblins and then eliminate orc with rocket launcher standing on the roof of the building at left [2].

Stairs across [1] leads you to the place, where you'll be shot by next orc's team. When you see enemies, hide behind rectangle mantle [2].

Your first goal should two orco giants with goggles [1]. Kill them with laser cannon. When everyone died, move left [3].

Next orc's team, with bomb-goggle appears, there [1]. Get rid of them using Vengeance launches [2].

Few metres onward you'll see a craft with enemies landing on the surface of the planet [1]. As first shoot down everyone you see with a sniper rifle, and then turn to the stairs on the left [2].

There starts appearing next vere [1]. They'll be in one big group, so a Vengeance launcher is the best choice [2].

Tunnel under the stairs leads to the small ammo store [1]. Few steps further is a big room with magazines' ammo inside it [2].

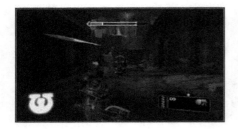

Standing in the doorway to the chamber, kill as fast as possible the gunners opposite [1] and blow out barrels on the left [2].

A moment later, elite ork's names begin to appear on the stairs [1]. Don't let them get close to you, shooting from Vengeance launcher. When it's done, take care of enemies on the balcony at left [2].

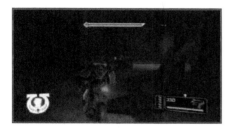

After fight, search the room. You'll find lot of box with ammo [1]. Pick all of them and run upstairs on the landing [2].

8 - Whispers of The Dead - p. 2
WH40K: Space Marine Guide

Last update: 11 May 2016

A moment later, on the upper floor enemies show up [1]. Kill them using Vengeance launcher and Laser Cannon [2].

Near to the place they were standing, you'll find ruins, which leads on the roof of the building [1]. Go upstairs and kill an enemy, who is hiding there [2].

Moving forward you'll reach square with monument [1], where inquisitor you were looking for, awaits [2].

When you finish talking with him, go to the corridor on the right [1]. Going straight, you'll get to the place where soldiers are fighting with charging orcs [2].

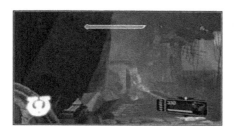

Don't move closer to them! Hide behind the corner instead, and start shooting to them [1]. Get rid of gunners with Laser Cannon, and those fighting hand to hand, eliminate with Vengeance launcher [2]. When the area gets clear, run to the soldiers and speak to them.

Without your team, move to the place marked with fist [1]. Moving upstairs, you'll reach a capsule with Jet Pack [2]. You'll also get new weapon - Thunderhammer.

Equipped that way fly to the right, moving over a stone wall [1]. On the left capsule with orcs will land [2].

Kill them all using powerful hammer, and move to the fist marked place [1]. After picking up ammo, which lays near to capsule, go upstairs and fly over the wall [2].

A moment later you'll be in a huge chamber, attacked by orcs with shaman [1]. Warlock should die first. Fly to him quickly and start hitting with thunderhammer [2]. Enemy will teleport form time to time, but with jet pack such chase shouldn't be a problem.

When shaman died, exterminate rest of orcs and move to the place marked by fist [1].

There'll be next ones - kill them. Hammer and jet pack will be very useful [2].

Moving forward you'll get to the chamber with second shaman [1]. Like previous time - kill him, and then take care about rest of company [2].

Fist marked road will take you to the soldier's camp [1]. Move to the helicopter pointed by lieutenant and the stage will end [2].

9 - The Weapon
WH40K: Space Marine Guide

Last update: 11 May 2016

You'll begin this chapter shooting from cannon to flying orcs [1]. Enemies appear from right, so keep looking that way. After a while, there'll be an orcs fall craft. Shoot them down, before they destroy your craft, and repeat it as many times, as many you'll be asked to [2].

Few minutes later hero will left this cannon. Now your task is eliminate orcs from backside of the craft [1]. When it's done, hide behind the wall to avoid being shot from Georgia [2]. Now shot to the enemy's craft until you'll be safe on the ground.

Just after landing you'll be attacked by the bunch of orcs [1]. After defeating first wave of enemies, shoot down those standing on towers [2]. When the last one charging foe died, come up to the red tower in the middle. You'll be taken to the rest of your comrades.

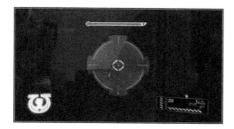

After the talk, move forward, and next turn right killing hordes of enemies [1]. Especially dangerous are gunners on upper platforms, so eliminate them first [2].

When you reach a destroyed bridge, turn right. Path will lead you to the landing place of our craft [1]. During an encounter, hide behind nearest rock and shoot down enemies armed in rocket launchers with sniper rifle. Those coming too close, kill with Thermal Rifle [2].

On the opposite end of battlefield, you'll find a little ammo [1]. Pick it up and turn right. Next path leads to crushed helicopter [2]. Replenish amount of ammo and go forward.

Killing revenants, you'll reach a small bridge over the abyss. An powerful army of enemies starts charging on you there. Defeat them using Fury or Thermal Rifle.

On the second side, move forward until you get to the closed gate [1]. When the detonator will try to open it, you have to fight with hordes of opponents. Before you attack, remember about taking Thunderhammer, which lays near to boxes with ammo [2].

After 2-3 waves of enemies, big group will attack form left flank. Amongst them are enemies with shields and powerful elite unites [1]. During the fight remember about using Fury, and when the gate are open, just run inside [2].

Inside, change a hammer on more hurtful weapon and follow your comrades [1]. When you go outside, don't come to far. After a moment groups of orcs appear - you'll have to get rid of them [2]. Especially look for the bombing creatures - it's easy to missed them in the mist.

When the first wave is eliminated, run forward killing next enemies [1]. After passing order the bridge full of orcs, you'll reach the place with flowing water [2].

Narrow path go upstairs, and move to the opposite side of iron sidewalk [1]. You'll get to the pits, which lead you to the next chapter [2].

10 - Mystery Skull
WH40K: Space Marine Guide

Last update: 11 May 2016

After beginning, run forward until you get to the closed gate [1]. Open it, turn left and hide behind containers [2]. You'll be shot by the guard tower hanging form the ceiling. To move on, you have to destroy it.

Behind next gate, more enemies waiting for you. Hide behind a barricade [1], and shoot down a turret from right, then from the left, and the middle one [2].

After entering the next room, run fast to the containers on the left [1]. Stealthing from one mantle to another, destroy turrets [2]. Ring that way all chamber.

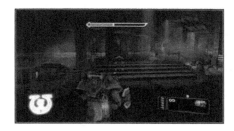

When you finish, go through the only one available gate [1]. After getting on the other side, pick up ammo [2].

It's be useful to destroy turrets moving along the corridor [1]. One is on the left, and one on the right [2].

There is chamber full of deadly machines behind the next gate. After entering, hide behind a mantle on the right and destroy two closest cannons [1]. When they blow out, run to the wall at left [2]. Behind it you'll be completely safe.

Sticking neck out for every few seconds, shoot down next enemies [1], and run after the minigun[2].

After opening the gate, run the gauntlet. The last one turret is there [1]. Still following your mysterious companion, you'll get to the container with Kraken Bolter [2]. This gun takes place of standard Bolter in your equipment. New weapon is great against heavy armored enemies, but in destroying turrets the best choice is Laser Cannon.

Armed, wait until inquisitor checks the core [1], and then go to the next chamber [2]. Hiding behind mantles, destroy all hidden cannons.

The only one available path will lead you to the corridor with three turrets. First on the left, second on the right and the last one at the end of the room.

Going through next gates, you'll get to the room with five machines [1]. All of them are on the opposite end of the chamber [2].

When you destroy them, move to the place pointed by the inquisitor [1]. There is a container with Purify Seal inside it [2]. Thanks to that, you access The Greatest Fury.

When the security systems shut down, go into the room with the generator [1]. A moment later ork's army appears [2]. Firstly eliminate gunners on sides, and then Take care about the rest. Keep them on distance, because there are suiciders among them.

After clearing up the room, come up to the machine in the center and pick inside it a source of energy [1]. A moment later alarm starts ringing. Run quickly to the gate and use elevator to get upstairs [2].

11 - Point of no Return
WH40K: Space Marine Guide

Last update: 11 May 2016

You'll get to the room with cables. Kill orcs you find inside [1] and bring the power back [2].

Nearest stairs leads you to a mechanism, which let you launch a powerful cannon [1]. A moment later forces of chaos show up [2].

When cut-scene ended, defeat small demon's squad [1] and get to the elevator [2].

Downstairs even more fighting is waiting for you, but enemies shouldn't be troublesome [1]. Moving forward and eliminating hordes of enemies, you'll get to the exit from the laboratory [2]. A while later stage ends.

12 - Dying of the Light - p. 1
WH40K, Space Marine Guide

Last update: 11 May 2010

When the stage begins, move to the place marked by pulsating fist [1] and jump into the wide pipe [2].

It'll lead you to the ruined complex [1]. On the crossroads turn right, and you reach room with blue container [2]. There is a Iron Halo hidden inside. It increases your armor a lot.

Outside you'll see a battle between orcs and forces of chaos [1]. Firstly eliminate shooting orcs and the demon's leaders [1]. When they died, take care about the rest creatures

When the fight is over, come up to the marked first place [ ]. Inside the building you'll
find ammo store, where you can replenish your supplies. Further path leads to the left. In
big chamber three demons-portal appear [2]. First part of enemies starts running from the
nearest one.

Gunners eliminate with grenades, and their leader by using sniper rifle [1]. When everyone's died, move closer and kill of demon's fighting hand to hand [2].

Next squads of chaos will come from the right [1]. Defeat them in the same way as previous, and go downstairs [2].

From the gate on the left some monsters will run into you [1]. Grind them down, listen to your Guardsman and move to the second side [2].

A bit further you'll see next fight between orcs and demons [1]. I advise to eliminate green snipes from the building on the left at the beginning [2].

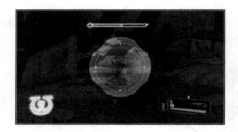

When they die, shoot down chaos leaders with a little help of Laser Cannon [1]. One headshot should be enough to kill an enemy [2].

After cleaning up, go onto the iron footbridge, which leads to a platform [1]. Launch mechanism, which is on it, and it begins going downstairs [2].

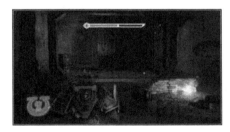

Downstairs talk to the lieutenant and go to the next room, filled with orcs [1]. Eliminate groups in sequence, stealthing from mantle to mantle [2].

That way you'll reach stairs, leading to the iron footbridge [1]. Kill orcs standing on it, and then run to the opposite side [2].

12 - Dying of the Light - p. 2
WH40K - Space Marine Guide

Last update: 11 May 2010

From behind a barricade, get prepared to charging waves of orcs [1]. There'll be almost all types of enemies amongst them, so be careful. When the place is clear, go into the elevator behind your back, which takes you upstairs [2]

Corridor will lead you outside [1], and iron pavement to the undergrounds of ruins [2].

There is a blue container with Plasma Rifle inside [1]. Pick up new weapon and go to the guardsmen defending in the trenches [2].

Help them to fight with orcs, replenishing your ammo during interludes between waves. When area is clear [1], move forward through the trench system [2].

You'll get to the orc's landing zone [1]. I recommend to use a Fury and get rid of them in few seconds [2].

A lot later little longer encounter awaits you. Hiding behind barricades, kill as fast as possible gunners, and then take care about those ones fighting hand to hand [1]. When area will be cleared, run quickly to the green diode in the middle of the plaza [2].

After launching feeding, the turrets get activated [1]. You can move back to the previous position and look on the massacre of your enemies [2].

Moving back more, you should see an entry to a building on the left [1]. Corridor leads you to the ammo store. Pick up everything and open the gate. Orc's leader will haul you inside the room [2].

Fight with him is long and difficult. At the beginning attack him with Thermical Cannon, until he hits the wall and first group of weaker orcs appears [1]. Use a Fury, which health you and make encounter easier. Repeat those things until the Leader jump on the platform [1]. From that place, he'll make two types of attacks. Both, rockets and grenades, avoid by making substractions. Additionally, great orc few times summons bomb squigs and weaker orcs. Kill them quickly, don't let them get close to you. During interlude between those attacks still shooting to the Leader. Extra ammo you'll find in chests near to the walls.

When the fight is over, get into the elevator and go upstairs [1]. There will be your comrades waiting for you. Get into the wagon with them and finish the chapter [2].

13 - Wake the Sleeping Giant
WH40K: Space Marine Guide

Last update: 11 May 2016

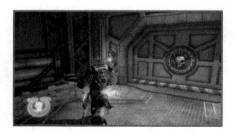

After going through the second gate, replenish ammo in the armory at left [1] and move forward [2].

A moment later you'll reach a big room, when forces of chaos will attack [1]. Hiding behind Barricades, try to shoot doors with super stronger enemies, and rest grind down using Bolter. When area is cleared, run to the place marked with fist [2].

After opening the second gate, hide behind the wall quickly [1]. You'll be shot from Heavy Bolter standing in the middle [2]. Kill soldier using it and don't let anyone else take it once more time. Other enemies shouldn't be troublesome. When everyone's dead, come up to the next gate.

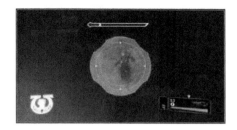

Creating portals wizard appears there [1]. Hide then behind the closest pillar and eliminate him with sniper rifle [2].

After killing the rest of enemies, you can go to the next chamber [1]. Inside, real sniper duel is waiting for you. Hide quickly behind some mantle and stick your neck out only for few seconds. You should see green laser [2]. Locate its source and kill enemy using Laser Cannon.

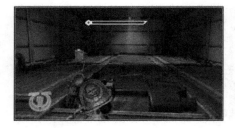

Repeat it until you get to the next gate [1]. There is an elevator behind it - it will take you on the lower floor [2].

Corridor devastates leads to the mechanism which activates Titan [1]. Launch that powerful machine, and go through the gate on the left [2].

Moving forward, you'll get to the big chamber, in which soldiers of chaos start appearing [1]. Hide behind the closest barrel, and start shooting [2].

When the last enemy died, move to the opposite side of the room. Appears there a demonic warrior [1]. The easiest way to defeat him, is using Thermal Rifle. To avoid his attacks, keep subversing. 4-5 shots should finish warrior [2].

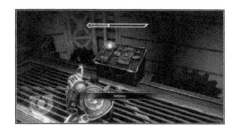

When fight your comrades go to the right, and you'll have to go through the central gate [1]. Corridor behind it leads to the moving platform. Launch it and move to the higher floor [2].

You'll get to the room with a container releasing a Titan [3]. Before you use it, go downstairs and open blue container [2]. There is a Storm Bolter inside it.

When the Titan is released, go through the next gate and with a new rifle, destroy flying turret [1]. Running forward you'll reach a platform which'll take you on the upper floor [2].

Moving forward you reach a titan, on which you can jump off [1]. When the captain of the machine stops talking, make few steps left, but don't go behind a corner [2].

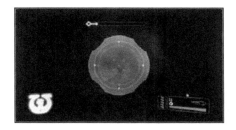

A moment later wizards start appearing in the air [1]. You have to shoot them down with Laser Cannon [2].

When you finish, flying turret will attack you. Shoot it down from Storm Bolter [1], and a stage will end [2].

14 - Victory and Sacrifice
WH40K: Space Marine Guide

Last update: 11 May 2016

Running forward, you'll reach place where chaos marine attacks [1]. Hide behind a throttle and kill everyone with Super Mode [2]. Remember to aim in head - if you get out of ammo, take some from box at the left.

When the fight is over, go through the gate on the left. There longer cut-scene begins [1]. After that, wizards will attack you [2].

You have to kill them ASAP, before they summon backup [1]. When it's done, eliminate armored soldiers of chaos [2].

At some point, also elite units will appear. Two powerful warriors start charging on you, so change weapon to Thermal Rifle and start shooting [1]. When enemies get to close, use Fury and finish them. When the last one died, a helicopter will land near to you. Short cut-scene introduce you to the next chapter [2].

15 - Prince of Daemons
WH40K - Space Marine Guide

Last update: 31 May 2016

When the stage begins, pick up ammunition located near to you[1], and use a mechanism, which lower an elevator [2].

Downstairs you'll find even more ammo [1]. A bit further, first encounter with chaos army awaits [2].

Hiding behind barrels [1], eliminate all gunners, and move forward. There'll be another team on the left [2].

When you shot, part of enemies change into red chaos demons [1]. Before they get to close to you, try eliminate as many as possible gunners [2]. Theirs grenades could be troublesome.

When area is cleared, go to the enemies position, pick up ammo, and turn left [1]. Far should wizards summoning chaos army starts appearing [2]. Take care about them with Laser Cannon.

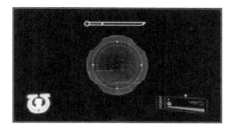

In the same way, get rid of foes with rocket Launchers [1] - rest of them kill from a Bolter [2].

At the end of the square turn right [1] and head for place marked with pulsating fist [2].

Next portal, from which chaos forces come out, appears there[1]. Kill all enemies and go inside [2]. In the corridor you'll find boxes with ammo and weapons.

At the end of the path, you'll be attacked by two enemies [1]. Kill them using Laser Cannon and jump down [2].

After landing go under the ruins on the right [1]. When you get to the second side, elite unit of chaos will run downstairs[2].

Standing by invisible "wall" you will be able to kill harmless enemy without any risk [1]. Remember to use Thermal Rifle or Laser Cannon [2].

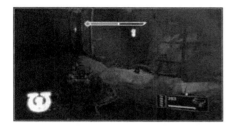

When he died, leave the ruins and go to the place marked with fist [1]. You'll be attacked by a small group of soldiers there [2].

When everyone has died, run to the end of corridor, where you can find ammo and weapons [1]. A bit further you'll be attacked one more time. Weaker enemies will shot from downstairs, but chaos warriors with rocket launchers appear upstairs[2].

Kill all of them and run one floor lower, taking up ammo you'll find[1]. Downstairs, hide behind a mantle and throw grenades to near standing Heavy Bolter [2].

Only when it's destroyed take care about charging demons [1]. After fight, go into the corridor behind a cannon [2].

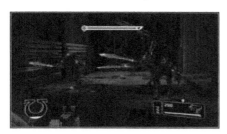

It leads you to the hall full of orcs [1]. Kill all of them, staying upstairs [2].

When you jump down, a creating portals wizard appears on the opposite side of the chamber[1]. Shot him down from a sniper rifle and take care about rest of demons [2].

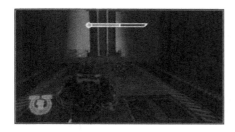

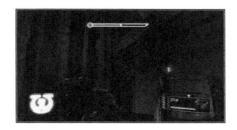

Moving forward you'll get to the platform [1], which takes you on upper floor [2]. You'll begin next stage there.

16 - Spire of Madness
WH40K - Space Marine Guide

Last update: 13 May 2016

At the beginning of the chapter go down along the iron footbridge and talk to one of Blood Ravens [1]. With a squad of them go right, killing next waves of enemies [2].

In some moment on your way portals from which demons start coming appear [1]. Kill enemies, hiding behind enemies and then eliminate wizards creating paths to the Abyss [1]. Make similar on the further way.

A bit later you'll find Autocannon Cannon [1]. Use it to eliminate charging enemies, especially for flying cannons [2].

When area get cleared [1], move to the craft of Ultra Marines, which takes you to the destroyed Spire [2].

After landing go forward, until you reach an edge [1]. There are enemies waiting for you on the other side - you'll easily kill them with hammer and Jet Pack. When last one died, fly to the platform in front of you [1]. During landing be careful, and don't fall down. It's south to run.

Kill enemies and jump on the edge of the LR [1]. A bit further a wizard you have to eliminate, quickly awaits you. When finished, defeat rest of foes, and fly left one more time [2].

Corridor leads to the next platform with enemies [1]. Further way go left [2].

After eliminating all enemies, Titus left a pack [1]. Onward you have to walk. Nearest corridor leads to the gate, before which you find ammo and weapons [2]. Change hammer

Inside, pick up your favorites rifles and open the gate. I advise to take Thermal Rifle and Laser Cannon.

Behind them flying cannon is waiting [1]. Destroy it with Laser Cannon, and turn left [2].

In a some moment you'll be attacked by team of demons and soldiers [1]. Firstly get rid of gunners, and then eliminate red creatures. When they day, go upstairs on ramp. Next army of enemies appears in front of you. Kill quickly wizard standing near to the portal [2], and after that shoot down armored foes.

Going forward you'll reach a platform, which could be launched by nearest mechanism [1]. In that way you get to the upper floor, where the last chapter begins [2].

17 - Man Against Demon

WH40K: Space Marine Guide

Last update: 11 May 2016

After meeting Nemeroth you'll be attacked by team of red demons [1]. They are very powerful, so use fury during the fight [2].

When they died, armored and equipped with rocket launchers enemies appeared [1]. Weaker ones eliminate with Bolter, and stronger from Laser Cannon. Remember about hiding behind the closest chests [2].

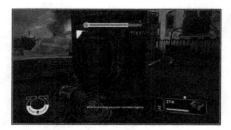

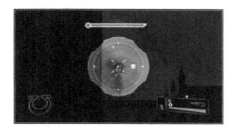

In third wave of enemies, red demons appear again, supported with powerful mages [1]. Red ones finish using Fury, and wizards shoot down with Laser Cannon [2].

When they died, there'll be the last one, the most dangerous, attack. Demons and enemies with hammers start charging on you [1]. It's best to use Thermal Rifle against them.

Moving back, shoot of your clip. If you run out of ammo, pick it up from boxes [2].

After this difficult fight, time will come for final battle with Nemeroth [1]. To defeat him, you have to press in proper moments buttons which will showed on the screen [2]. If you make mistake, you'll lose part of hit points.

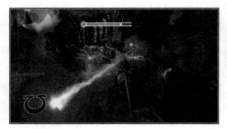

Besides, demons will shot violet missiles [1]. Avoid them, flying round. Battle is not easy, but keys combos are repeatable, so after few tries you should win it. When Nemeroth died, the game is over [2]. Congratulations!

Chapter 2
WH40K: Space Marine Guide

Last update: 11 May 2016

Shift Journal 1/5

In chapter Against Everything, you'll get to the low fault. Jump down and shoot down enemies standing on the left [1]. A bit further there is a crossroads. The path to right leads to first skull probe [2].

Shift Journal 2/5

After finding Leandros [1] and defeating attacking orcs, move forward. Just before the entry to the bunker system, there is second skull probe [2].

Medical Journal 3/5

After leaving bunker with lieutenant, you'll be attacked by orcs - they came out from underground schacht [1]. Defeat all of them and go to the bunker on the right. Inside it you'll find skull probe [2].

Lieutenant's Mira Journal 1/5

After collecting Hunter Bolter and eliminating orcs with it, you'll reach corridor under the ruins. In some moment orc start throwing grenades to you [1]. Kill him and turn left. Near to the ammo box, you'll find next skull probe [2].

Guardsman Journal 2/5

After collecting previous skull probe, move forward until you find next enemies [1]. Kill charging orcs and gobbins, and then get inside the bunker on the left [2]. There you'll find an item you are looking for.

Chapter 3
W1140K Space Marine Guide

Last update: 11 May 2016

Shift Journal 1/5

After reaching the fortress look carefully to the wall at right [1]. There is a passage to small room with skull probe inside [2].

Lieutenant's Mira Journal 2/5

After visiting armory you'll go by elevator to the big hangar [1]. Skull probe is across the

Session [2]

Chapter 4
WH40K - Space Marine Guide

Last update: 11 May 2016

Medical Journal 2/5

When you see ramp [1], go to the opposite end of the hangar, and turn left. There is a skull on the behind a wall [2].

Chapter 5
WH40K - Space Marine Guide

Last update: 11 May 2016

Guardsman Journal 3/5

When you finish fighting with the first orc's team on this stage, stay in front of entrance to the next hangar [1]. You should see skull probe and box with ammo behind your back[2].

Inquisition Report 1/5

Second skull probe you'll find just at the end of the chapter. When elevator goes down, move forward. [1] Over one of the chests you should see the item you need [2].

Chapter 6

WH40K: Space Marine Guide

Last update: 11 May 2016

Shift Journal 2/5

After going up with elevator and confirming inquisitor presence [1], walk downstairs and go through the open gate. You should see skull probe on the left[2].

Inquisition Report 2/5

When you get to the fabric hall with orcs coming out form pipes, move forward. Just before exit, which is marked by dot, there is small crossroads [1]. Go path on the left, and you'll find a recording [2].

Chapter 7

Witcher: Space Marine Guide

Last update: 11 May 2016

Shift Journal 2/5

Inside one of corridors you'll be attacked by two waves of enemies with elite unit among them. When the fight ended, go to the end of the room [1]. Tunnel on the right leads to the next stage of mission, this on the left to the skull probe [2].

Medical Journal 3/5

After collecting Thermal Rifle and defeating orc's army, move forward until you reach high fault [1]. Downstairs, on the left, is small barricade - behind it next skull probe is localized with a small amount of ammo.

Chapter 8
WH40K: Space Marine Guide

Last update: 11 May 2016

Medical Journal 4/5

When you go inside the first building, corridor leads you to the hole in the floor [1]. Jump down, and turn around about 180 degrees. You should see then first skull probe on this level [2].

Inquisition Report 3/5

After taking Laser Cannon and defeating group of orcs, go inside the corridor marked with fist[1]. Few steps from entrance, turn to the room on the right You'll find second skull probe inside it[2].

Shift Journal 3/5

The next one is hidden in the room on the first floor. It's on the left from corridor.

Personal Message 1/5

After defeating orks who descends in shaft capsule, go downstairs and inside the tunnel under ruins [1]. Moving forward look carefully to the wall on the right side of corridor. You'll find there entrance to the small room with ammo and skull probe inside it[2].

Inquisition Report 4/5

Tunnel leads to the small ammo storage - there is a big room with orcs behind it[1]. After defeating all enemies, go upstairs and search this floor - you'll find another skull probe [2].

Personal Message 2/5

When you pick up a Jet Pack, fly on the nearest rise and fly further this direction [1]. On the next floor you'll find skull probe [2].

Inquisition Report 5/5

After collecting jet pack and defeating team of enemies, go to the marked with fist direction [1]. Behind one's capsule are stairs, and to the right of them you'll see a recording [2].

Shift Journal 4/5

When you defeat teleportating orc's shaman [1], search a right site of the chamber. One passage leads to the room with skull probe [2].

Drogan's Journal 1/10

After collecting previous recording, go to the marked with last direction. You'll get to the small crossroads [1]. Path on the left leads to an item you are looking for [2].

Shift Journal 5/5

Still running to the list, you'll find another crossroads. This time, go right [1]. Jumping between levels, look at the wall on the left. In some moment you should see a hole - fly through it [2].

You'll land near to the benches and a statue [1]. There is a skull probe near to the sculpture[2].

Chapter 9
WH40K: Space Marine Guide

Last update: 11 May 2016

Personal Message 3/5

When you meet again with the inquisitor and two comrades, run forward and turn right. You'll be attacked by orcs' team. Killing those creatures you'll reach broken bridge [1]. On the left you should see a breach in rocks - there is hidden skull probe [2].

Medical Journal 5/5

When you get to the second side of bridge, move forward, until you reach destroyed helicopter [1]. There is recording near to its front[2].

Lieutenant's Mira Journal 3/5

When you get to the entrance to pits, go back downstairs, and search carefully terrain next to place where water falls from big pipe [1]. There is a skull probe between rocks[2].

Chapter 10
WH40K - Space Marine Guide

Last update: 11 May 2016

Shift Journal 3/5

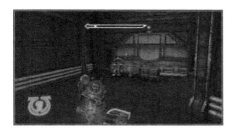

After destroying turrets moving along the corridor [1], move forward to the first crossroads (to right and you'll find a skull probe [2].

Shift Journal 4/5

When you get Kraken Bolter, go to the next room and destroy all cannons inside it [1]. When it's done search room at right [2].

You'll have to destroy another power node it [1]. After that, pick up recording laying near to it [2].

Drogan's Journal 2/10

The first one skull probe you'll find on the right from the place you have to use source of energy [1]. It's near to the burning gate [2].

Chapter 12
WH40K: Space Marine Guide

Last update: 11 May 2016

Personal Message 4/5

After beginning a chapter move forward, and jump into the wide pipe. You'll get to the crossroads - turn right. Behind a barricade, which can be blow up [1], first skull probe is[2].

Drogan's Journal 3/10

Second recording you'll find in room with Iron Halo [1]. It's hidden between ruins in left corner of the chamber [2].

Lieutenant's Mira Journal 4/5

When you eliminate first squads of fighting orcs and demons, go to the place marked by fist. There a stairs inside a room, which leads on upper floor [1]. Turn right and search bedrooms [2]. In of them another skull probe is.

Guardsman Journal 4/5

When you meet lieutenant, go to the next room and kill orcs inside it [1]. There is recoming on the opposite side of hall[2].

Drogan's Journal 4/10

After meeting with lenter, you'll go to upper floor by elevator. Running forward look at the wall on the right [1]. There'll be an entrance to the small room with skull probe inside[2].

Shift Journal 5/5

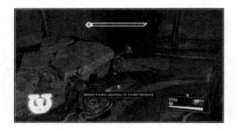

Next recording can be found near to the container with Plasma Rifle [1]. It hovers in the corner of the room [2].

Guardsman Journal 5/5

At some moment you and your comrades part looking for a generator responsible for barrier. Path leads to trenches where ten soldiers are standing [1]. There are boxes with ammo and skull probe right to them.

Lieutenant's Mira Journal 5/5

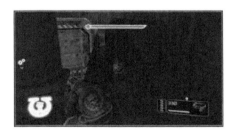

After launching turrets, make few steps back and go inside a building on the left [1]. At the end of corridor you'll find small ammo store. Behind boxes skull probe is hidden[2].

Chapter 13
WH40K: Space Marine Guide

Last update: 11 May 2016

Drogan's Journal 5/10

When first encounter with chaos forces is finished, search left wall of the room mindfully[1]. There'll be an entrance to the chamber with hovering recording [2].

Drogan's Journal 6/10

After fight with snipers, go downstairs using elevator [1]. At the bottom on the left you'll find skull probe [2]

Drogan's Journal 7/10

At same stage of a mission you and your comrades will part. Two move right, and you should go through the middle gate [1]. Before that, check out corridor on the left. It leads to the room, inside which there is another skull probe [2].

Possession 1/3

After releasing a Titan, go through the closest gate and destroy flying turret [1]. Going forward you'll reach small crossroads. Go left and you'll find next recording [2].

Chapter 15
WH40kc Space Marine Guide

Last update: 11 May 2016

Drogan's Journal 8/10

First skull probe you can find at the beginning of a chapter. Go downstairs with elevator [1]. recording is hovering near, on your right [2].

Personal Message 5/5

After fight with hammer-armed enemy, go forward until you reach an entrance to tunnels [1]. Few soldiers will attack you there. Kill them and search carefully rubbles behind big piece of scrap-iron [2]. There is skull probe hide in.

Possession 2/3

After destroying Heavy Bolter, go into the corridor behind it [1]. Already on the first turn you'll find boxes with ammo and skull probe [2].

Chapter 16
WH40K: Space Marine Guide

Last update: 11 May 2016

Drogan's Journal 9/10

When equipped with Jet Pack you kill first demonic wizard, fly left [1]. There is a recording inside this corridor [2].

Drogan's Journal 10/10

Near to the previous skull probe, demons attack you [1]. Kill them and fly on the platform behind them. After eliminating enemy standing on it, you can pick about another recording [2].

Possession 3/3

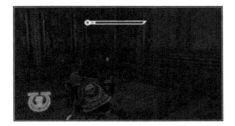

After Titus throw out Jet Pack, move forward [1]. At the end of corridor there is a gate - behind it flying cannon will attack you. When you destroy it, turn left and pick up the last one recording [2].

ABOUT THE AUTHOR

Thank you for reading book.